Also by Raymond Britt

Chicago Marathon: Images of Sports

Ironman Lake Placid: Racing Tips and Strategies

Racing Ironman: From Debut to Kona and Beyond

Racing Ironman Wisconsin: Everything You Need to Know

Epic Cycling: Riding The Legendary Ironman Bike Course

Qualifying for Kona: The Road to Ironman Triathlon World Championship

Front Cover: Finishers crossing the line at the 2008 Boston Marathon.

Boston Marathon: The Legendary Course Guide

By Raymond Britt

Published by RunTriMedia Publishing
Chicago IL, Scottsdale AZ, Boston MA

Second Printing

10001025600324101000

1 2 3 4 5 6 7 8 9 0 9 8 7 6 5 4 3 2 1 13 1000

Printed in the United States of America

Visit us at www.RunTriMedia.com and www.RaymondBritt.com

For Mom, Wendy, Amanda, Rebecca, Eric and Kirsten

Contents

Acknowledgments

My invaluable team of training, racing and supporting partners have included Steve Abbey, Art Hutchinson, Joe Foster, Warren Helfman, Jean-Paul Ruiz-Funes, Tom Flickinger, Bill Hague Patrick McHugh, Bob Mina, Paul Zellner, Barry Schliesmann, Kathy Winkler, Lisa Smith-Batchen, Michael Fisch, Marc Roy at SportStats Timing, Vinu Malik at xtri.com, Jesse Williams and Steve DeKoker at Brooks Sports, Adam Greene at Scott Bikes, Tim Moxey at Nuun, Rob Sleamaker at VasaTrainer, Jeff Banowetz at Competitor Magazine, and many more. I thank you one and all for the exceptional experiences we've shared so far.

Special thanks to the Boston Athletic Association, Boston Marathon volunteers, and the spectators that line the legendary course from Hopkinton to Boston.

My Mother, Wendy, Amanda, Rebecca, Eric and Kirsten have encouraged, inspired, shared and celebrated the journey with me from the beginning. This book is dedicated to them with unending love and thanks.

Introduction

The Legendary Boston Marathon: the oldest, grandest and most exclusive marathon in the world. Millions aspire to run Boston, but only 25,000 meet the strict qualifying standards to run a course that is considered one of the toughest in the world.

If you're planning to race Boston, you had better know what you're up against. The course may look innocent, but as experts will tell you, it can be brutal. If you're not ready, if you don't understand the intricacies of the course, Boston can eat you alive.

This book takes the reader deep into the race course with a groundbreaking approach: a comprehensive mile-by-mile tour of the course illustrated with nearly 200 photos taken while running the race, complete race splits from seven different Boston races and the strategy implications for your race preparation.

From Hopkinton to Wellesley to Heartbreak Hill to the finish line, this book delivers the complete experience in images, analytics and advice to help you run a great Boston Marathon.

My Boston debut was in 1996, and while it was not pretty, it was the first of 13 consecutive epic races on the legendary course.

During these 13 years of running Boston, I've had an exceptionally wide variety of experiences on the course. One thing I know for sure after all those years: Boston is unpredictable, and I have the scars and personal bests to prove it.

If you're like most rookies preparing for your first Boston, or if you're returning with a goal of racing well, you are looking for more detailed insight into the course to help you have a great race. You want to know what the entire Boston experience is like -- what to expect, elevation, speed, rough spots, fast sections, how to race it, how to survive it, how to overcome obstacles, how to have a great finish it, and how to celebrate your success. That's what this book is all about.

The first chapter provides a broad overview of what you can expect at the Boston Marathon. It's the big picture, the story of what you will experience on race day. Adapted from one of the most popular articles published at RunTri.com, it's designed to provide context for the detailed course analysis in this book.

The second chapter zeroes in on runner's race pace for a variety of finish times, and also illustrates good and poor race pace strategies.

In this chapter, the mile-by-mile splits from six of my Boston Marathon races are presented for comparison and analytic perspective. From a 3:41 in 1996 to my PR of 2:54 in 2002, you'll see that understanding the course and applying the right strategy are essential at Boston.

Most of my races in Boston have varied to some degree, from good, to bad, to ugly. The lessons from the splits are revealing, demonstrating the outcomes of different strategies on the challenging course.

The mile-by-mile splits help illustrate strategies and misfires, and provide real examples of what can happen at each section of the course. More important, they help the reader understand the relationship between race pace, mile-by-mile, and the complexity of the course as shown in the race photos.

Finally, the bulk of this book is devoted to a complete, in-depth look at each mile of Boston Marathon course. For years, I've heard from runners who want to know more about the Boston course, beyond the course map and elevation charts. The charts are helpful, but limited. Another resource, the 3-minute time-lapse driving-the-course videos shown at race expos, also has not been very helpful to envision the real race experience.

I kept thinking there had to be a better way to understand the course. So, beginning in 2005, I started photographing the Boston race experience. Each year since, I've shot photos of one or more major angles of the race.

In 2005 and 2006 I shot photos of the race morning, starting, finishing and post-finish parts of the race. In 2007 and 2008, I ran Boston with a camera in hand, shooting hundreds of photos from various spots on the course while running 4-hour marathons. In 2009, I shot an extensive collection of photos of the elite and First Wave start and finish.

With 13 years experience running Boston and a complete archive of photos capturing every aspect of the race, this book is intended to be an ultimate course tour with the goal of helping you know what to expect on race day, how to run the race smartly, and, most of all, to have your best ever Boston Marathon experience.

The Boston Marathon Experience:
What to Expect

More than 20,000 runners compete in the Boston marathon, including thousands who will be competing for the first time. There is nothing like it in the world. You'll know what I mean when you get there. Here's what you can expect.

Race Morning

The excitement of race day begins with a dawns-early light procession of thousands of runners heading toward the buses that will transport them to the race start. I prefer to get on one of the earlier buses to get settled in Hopkinton, but there's no real advantage to an early or a late boarding time. With two staging areas at Hopkinton High School for runners to relax before the race, there's plenty of space for everyone.

The bus ride from downtown Boston to Hopkinton always seems long, long enough to make you realize that 26 miles is quite a distance to run. As if you didn't know that already. But it is a little intimidating, still.

There can also be a small delay between the time your bus enters Hopkinton and arrives at the high school, as it takes time to empty each bus in order. I only mention this because it happens every year: a long bumpy bus ride with dozens of runners constantly hydrating inevitably leads to one or more who beg the bus driver to make an unscheduled stop for emergency bladder relief. Lesson: everyone, as we tell our kids before long trips -- go before you leave.

Once in the Athlete Village, find a spot, and relax. People bring all sorts of things, from blow-up chairs, to blankets, to plastic bags to newspapers. Bring what you like, just expect it to be disposable. If it's a rainy morning, you may want to wear an old pair of shoes in the potentially muddy village, and change to your dry race shoes later.

It can be chilly in the early morning, and my preference is to wear fleece to stay warm. In the past, a noon start meant the rising sun would warm the area late in the morning. With a 10am start, and runners moving to the start area soon after 9am, it's probably a good idea to wear a plastic cover or old clothes to stay warm until the start.

The Race

Standing on Main Street in your race corral just minutes before the starting gun, take it all in: helicopters whirring above, TV cameras panning the runners, spectators lined up deep along the narrow roadway, the singing of the Star-Spangled Banner complete with an Air Force flyover, and of course, the natural buzz of excitement from all the runners around you. Prepare to experience the greatest marathon there is.

Hopkinton. Unless you are right behind the elite runners, do not expect to begin running swiftly immediately after the starting gun. Main Street is very narrow, and there's little room to move.

You will likely walk across the start line before you start shuffling, then slowly begin running on a steep descent. The good news is that you can't run too fast downhill because you are so close to other runners, so you won't beat your legs early on.

Instead, enjoy what I think is one of the most amazing images in marathons: looking downhill to see thousands of heads bobbing up and down Main Street for as far as you can see.

Let yourself settle into a groove through the first 5k of net downhill road. Not that you won't experience some small rolling hills; you will. That's actually a good thing. It lets your legs stretch out and work a variety of muscles.

Ashland. You will briefly pass through Ashland for a couple of miles. Mile 3 is nearly all slightly downhill; just make sure not to overdo it in your early race excitement. You'll pay later if you run too fast here. Mile 4 actually takes you slightly uphill, and it's a good chance to even out your running pace. It's at this point that I usually lock in to a pace/mile that sticks for the next several miles.

Framingham. The main landmark in Framingham is the train station and large crowds greeting runners at about the 10k point. Miles 5 and 6 approaching this destination have continued to roll gently downhill with some brief inclines. but by now you're under control. Enjoy the crowd in Framingham -- wave, high five and smile. You won't see many people for three more miles.

Natick. Some peace on the road at this point is not a bad thing. After all the excitement from early morning through the first few miles, now it's time to do what you do best: run. The course is calm, gently rolling, but not difficult. Near the 15k mark, you will pass the Natick landmark: the clock tower and Natick Town Common. Crowds will be waiting, waving you on your way to Wellesley.

Wellesley. After Natick, the next two miles are again largely without spectators. Again, time to stay in control and appreciate your surroundings. Because when you get to Mile 12, the real race really starts.

There is nothing like the Screaming Women of Wellesley College. Sure, you've read about them, but you have to be there to experience it. The screaming is so overpowering, in a fun way, that I steered clear left away from all the fuss in my first few Bostons. But in recent years, I've decided to join the fun, running close to the crowd, taking it all in. You should too. Because after that, it's all uphill. Sort of.

Shortly after Wellesley College, you will reach the 13.1 mile point in downtown Wellesley. It will be gut-check time: how do you feel? Did you hold enough in reserve to handle the hills that will soon greet you? You will have miles 14 and 15 that roll ever so gently and slightly uphill through tree-lined neighborhoods to sort that all out. Then it's one steep roller coaster ride downhill approaching mile 16, and then it all begins.

Newton. The famous hills of the Boston Marathon really begin just before the 16 mile mark. There's a solid incline as the road approaches and crosses the 95/128 freeway. The spectators will begin narrowing to see runners, until there's a small gap to run through as you cross the bridge. They will be telling you 'you look great!' and you will begin wondering if you can handle the rest of the hills. Be confident: sure you can.

Because, surprisingly, the next hill doesn't come at you for another mile and a half. Not bad at all, really. You just keep running under control, and when you see the crowds getting thicker, prepare for a solid right hand turn at the Newton Fire Station to begin a steady climb. The crowds will cheer, you will smile as you put your head down and chug up this hill. It's about 3/8 of a mile long, not too terrible. I just run at the side of the road, keeping my eyes on the white stripe on the road, not looking for the top. When I get there, I get there.

And when you reach the top of that hill, again a surprise awaits. It's more than a mile to the next hill, and most of that is downhill, to boot. In fact, by this time, you will begin wondering what all this talk about the Hills of Boston was all about. Your main challenge at this point will be similar to your other marathons: handling getting through mile 19 with enough left in your tank to finish.

The third Newton Hill arrives at about mile 19.25, and is a little deceptive. Not particularly steep, it just keeps going longer than you expect. At 19.5, you will think you've crested the climb, but it's a brief respite. There's more to go. Stay with it.

And soon, you're at mile 20. 10k to go, the fun part. The real challenge awaits: the final Newton Hill, your path to mile 21. You will hear the climb before you actually get there. The roar of the crowd, combined with a pounding of drums, tells you that It's Almost Here.

You will see the gentle turn ahead, you will veer in that direction, then you will see an incline that simply disappears into the trees above. You will not see the top. Keep your head down, stay focused on the road. Again, I get to the side of the pavement, and keep my eyes on the road's white stripe, and just keep moving. Just tell yourself that in a few short minutes it will be over, and you'll be on your way to the finish.

When you get near the top, you will know it. Literally, a clearing seems to open up, and you can begin to see daylight. After a small dip, which you'll hope signal the end, there's another small incline then the hard part is over. You're on top of the backside of the course, and you'll be able to see downtown Boston in the distance, just before you fly (or not) downhill towards Boston College.

Brookline. Miles 22, 23 and 24 on their way though Brookline towards Boston are each net downhill, but that doesn't mean the course won't toss you a slight curveball here and there in the form of gentle inclines that frustrate the mind and body ever so irritatingly.

As my body is wearing down in those final miles, I start thinking that the finish line can't come soon enough. And these little jabs by the course inclines seem much more potent than they should be.

Boston. But by mile 25, all is forgiven, and you can begin to feel the finish line. The course flattens out once you cross the bridge by Fenway Park and the Citgo sign, and you know it's over soon. Take the last mile to savor where you are -- on hallowed ground, following the footsteps of 111 years of marathoners.

The most special part of the course, for me, is the right turn onto Hereford Street, followed by the left turn shortly afterwards onto Boylston, with the finish banner in the distance. There's a calm before the elation on quiet Hereford Street, shaded from the sun, isolated from the intense spectator cheers that await just seconds away.

The turn onto Boylston Street puts you in full view of what I believe is the greatest final stretch that you can experience in a marathon. Nearly a half mile of smiles waves and cheers from spectators on both sides of the street.

The finish banner, an unparalleled sight, comes into view. Take a deep breath, appreciate every stride that takes you closer to the Boston Marathon Finish banner. You worked hard to get to this point. You're there. Enjoy it.

As you run those final strides to the finish line, begin celebrating your own personal independence. You trained for months or even years to get to this point. And there you will be. Completing something that you once considered impossible, even ridiculous. A marathon, 26.2 miles. But not just any marathon. The legendary Boston Marathon.

Then it's your moment. See the time, cross the line, smile for the cameras. Congratulate yourself, be proud. You've done it. Go ahead, admit it to yourself: you Really Rock. You're a Boston Finisher. Yes, you are.

You've done something extraordinary, celebrate it. Celebrate your independence, celebrate your spirit and attitude that earned that trip to Hopkinton and drove you the next 26.2 miles to the most coveted finisher's medal in long-distance running.

In the Long Run, life is a collection of Moments That Matter. The ones you will remember for the rest of your life. In April, your moment is in Boston, on Boylston Street, under the Finish Banner.

That moment is yours. Celebrate it. From that moment on, you are a little more special. You are Boston finisher. Congratulations. Welcome to the Club.

Running the Course:
Maps, Splits and Race Pace Strategies

Boston Marathon Course Map

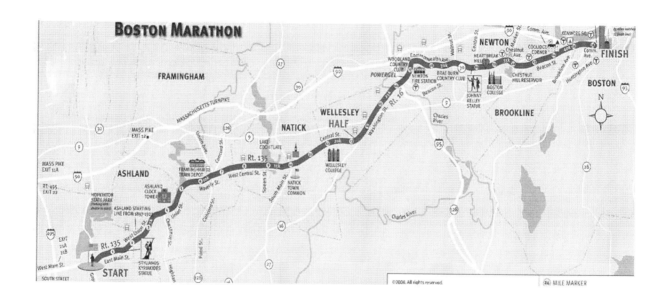

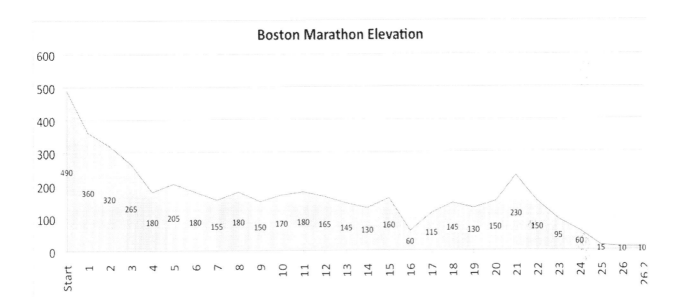

Boston Marathon Elevation

Course Geography

Mile	Km	City	Location	Milestone	Elevation	Change
Start	Start	**Hopkinton**	Main St.	Starting Line	490	n/a
1	1.6	Hopkinton	Rte. 135-East Main St.		360	-130
2	3.2	Ashland	Rte. 135-West Union St.	Starting Line 1897 to 1923	320	-40
3	4.8	Ashland	Rte. 135-East Union St.		265	-55
4	6.4	Ashland	Rte. 135-Union St.	Ashland Clock Tower	180	-85
5	8.0	Framingham	Rte. 135-Waverly St.		205	25
6	9.7	Framingham	Rte. 135-Waverly St.		180	-25
7	11.3	Framingham	Rte. 135-Waverly St.	Framingham Train Depot	155	-25
8	12.9	Natick	Rte. 135-West Central St.		180	25
9	14.5	Natick	Rte. 135-West Central St.		150	-30
10	16.1	Natick	Rte. 135-West Central St.	Lake Cochituate	170	20
11	17.7	Natick	Rte. 135-East Central St.	Natick Town Common	180	10
12	19.3	Wellesley	Rte. 135-Central St.		165	-15
13	20.9	Wellesley	Rte. 135-Central St.	Wellesley College	145	-20
14	22.5	Wellesley	Rte. 135-Central St.	Downtown Wellesley	130	-15
15	24.1	Wellesley	Rte. 16-Washington St.		160	30
16	25.7	Wellesley	Rte. 16-Washington St.	Wellesley Hills	60	-100
17	27.4	Newton Lower Falls	Rte. 16-Washington St.	95/128 Overpass	115	55
18	29.0	Newton	Rte. 16-Washington St.	Newton Fire Station	145	30
19	30.6	West Newton	Rte. 30-Commonwealth Ave.	Johnny Kelley Statue	130	-15
20	32.2	Newton	Rte. 30-Commonwealth Ave.	Second Newton Hill	150	20
21	33.8	Newton	Rte. 30-Commonwealth Ave.	Heartbreak Hill	230	80
22	35.4	Brookline	Rte. 30-Commonwealth Ave.	Boston College	150	-80
23	37.0	Brookline	Rte. 30-Commonwealth Ave.	Cleveland Circle	95	-55
24	38.6	Brookline	Rte. 9A-Beacon St.	Coolidge Corner	60	-35
25	40.2	Boston	Rte. 9A-Beacon St.	Boston University	15	-45
26	41.8	Boston	Rte. 9A-Beacon St.	Citgo Sign/Fenway Park	10	-5
26.2	42.2	Boston/Back Bay	Boylston St.	Boylston St.	10	0

Race Summaries and Mile-by-Mile Splits

I've never been able to run a negative split marathon, in Boston or during any of the other 80 marathons I've run. But when I'm able to run the second half of a marathon around 5% slower than the first half, I consider it a good race.

Before each Boston Marathon, I've taken stock of my fitness, confidence, desire and external considerations like weather to map a rough strategy for my race.

Based on my experience and expectations, I plan race strategy with the same rule of thumb: whatever my target is, I expect the second half to be roughly 5% slower. It works for me, but it's important that you ultimately choose targets based on what's right for you given your goals, fitness and other useful advice.

With those overall parameters set, step two is to set objectives for every 5k mark on the course. Key to setting the objectives and mapping strategy to meet the targets, depends on a thorough understanding of the course, personal history of both well- and poorly executed strategy.

Knowing the problem spots on the course allows for more practical and realistic objectives and strategy. And we have the experience and data to show you.

Depending on the year, I have run Boston with just about every outcome, from 2:54:37 to 4:42:11, ranging from fast (2002, for example), reasonably well (2002, 2004, 2005), conservative and steady (1996, 2007 and 2008) and flat out wrong (1997, 2001).

Because of the variety of successes and failures, important lessons can be illustrated by comparing races, and we'll apply the lessons throughout.

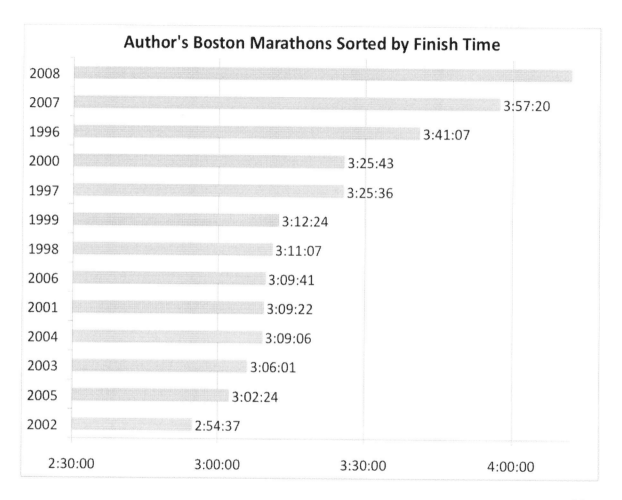

Author's Boston Marathons Sorted by Finish Time

Year	Finish Time
2008	
2007	3:57:20
1996	3:41:07
2000	3:25:43
1997	3:25:36
1999	3:12:24
1998	3:11:07
2006	3:09:41
2001	3:09:22
2004	3:09:06
2003	3:06:01
2005	3:02:24
2002	2:54:37

2:30:00   3:00:00   3:30:00   4:00:00

Success vs. Disappointment. Experts will tell you that going out too fast is a mistake. We agree. But what's too fast? Well, this is what 'too fast' compared to 'just right' looks like.

A perfect example is a comparison of my races in 2001 and 2002. Same racer, same potential, different execution, 15 minute difference in finish times at the end. The key: about 30 seconds/mile too aggressive in Ashland, miles 2, 3, and 4. That's it. Huge.

Boston Marathon Comparison: 2001 vs. 2002 Pace Per Mile

···2001 Finish Time 3:09:22   ▬2002 Finish Time 2:54:37

Benchmark Splits for Disappointing Race. More examples of disappointing execution exist in my Boston experience, unfortunately. But you can learn from the pattern that is obvious: too fast, too bad. It's notable that 1997 and 2001 finish times were Boston PRs at the time.

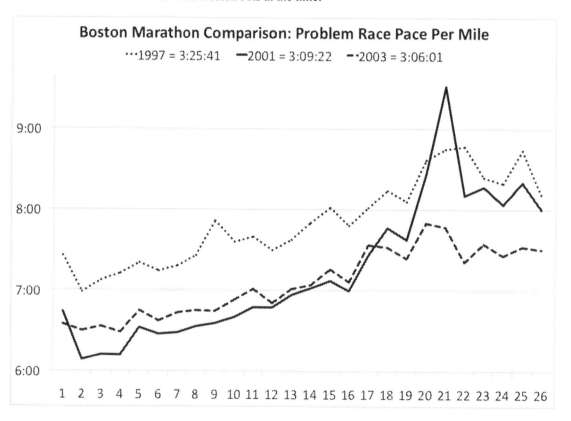

Boston Marathon Comparison: Problem Race Pace Per Mile
···1997 = 3:25:41   —2001 = 3:09:22   — ·2003 = 3:06:01

Benchmark Splits for Successful Races. The next year, I found out. One year smarter, more conservative, I ran solid races with, what for me, seems to be nearly perfect execution. Your expectations may vary but this is roughly the pattern you want to see, whether you want to run a 2:54, a 3:12 or a 3:41.

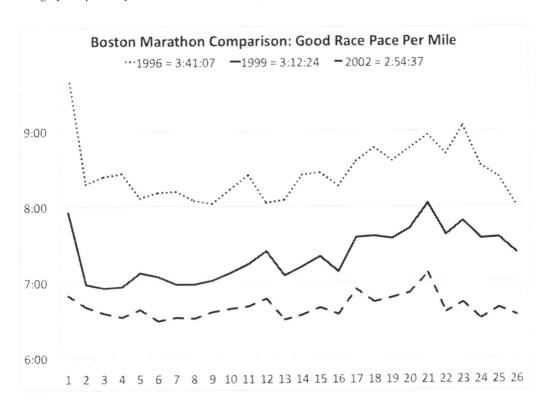

Boston Marathon Comparison: Good Race Pace Per Mile
····1996 = 3:41:07   —1999 = 3:12:24   ‒ 2002 = 2:54:37

Course Race Pace Lessons

Seems I've been through all the stages of running Boston: fast, slow, injured, running just for fun. The course stays the same, my way of dealing with it does not.

The way you approach the course is everything. Know what's out there. Know what to expect. Prepare strategies for a range of scenarios. Be ready to tackle the challenges as they come. Because they will come. But your preparation will get you through in the best way possible.

The rest of this book is designed to do exactly that. At the start of every main section of the course, Hopkinton, Ashland, etc., overviews, mile splits for these well-run and disappointing examples are included. So you can see suggested splits in different race scenarios.

With expectations defined in chapter one, and benchmark targets defined in this chapter, it's time to take in onto the course.

Author's Boston Marathon Details -- Selected Years				Benchmark Splits		
Mile	City	Elevation	Change	1996	1999	2002
Start	Hopkinton	490	n/a			
1	Hopkinton	360	-130	9:48	7:55	6:49
2	Ashland	320	-40	8:17	6:58	6:40
3	Ashland	265	-55	8:23	6:55	6:35
4	Ashland	180	-85	8:26	6:56	6:32
5	Framingham	205	25	8:06	7:07	6:38
6	Framingham	180	-25	8:10	7:04	6:29
7	Framingham	155	-25	8:11	6:58	6:32
8	Natick	180	25	8:04	6:58	6:31
9	Natick	150	-30	8:02	7:01	6:36
10	Natick	170	20	8:13	7:07	6:39
11	Natick	180	10	8:24	7:14	6:40
12	Wellesley	165	-15	8:02	7:24	6:46
13	Wellesley	145	-20	8:05	7:05	6:30
14	Wellesley	130	-15	8:24	7:12	6:34
15	Wellesley	160	30	8:26	7:20	6:40
16	Wellesley	60	-100	8:16	7:08	6:34
17	Newton Lower Falls	115	55	8:35	7:35	6:54
18	Newton	145	30	8:46	7:36	6:44
19	West Newton	130	-15	8:36	7:34	6:47
20	Newton	150	20	8:45	7:42	6:51
21	Newton	230	80	8:56	8:02	7:07
22	Brookline	150	-80	8:41	7:37	6:36
23	Brookline	95	-55	9:03	7:48	6:43
24	Brookline	60	-35	8:32	7:34	6:31
25	Boston	15	-45	8:23	7:35	6:39
26	Boston	10	-5	8:00	7:23	6:34
26.2	Boston/Back Bay	10	0	1:32	1:36	1:26
Finish Time				3:41:07	3:12:24	2:54:37

**Tour of the
Legendary
Course**

Tour Guide

- **Race Morning**

- **Athletes' Village**

- **Race Start**

- **Hopkinton**

- **Ashland**

- **Framingham**

- **Natick**

- **Wellesley**

- **Newton**

- **Brookline**

- **Boston**

Race Morning

6:45am, leaving the hotel at Copley Square, beginning the walk to Boston Common.

I make it a point to stop by the finish line with friends on Boylston before walking east to the Boston Common. **B.A.A 5K:** the newly instituted B.A.A. 5k is run here on Sunday.

From the finish line to the bus lines in Boston Common, plan on at least a 10-minute brisk walk.

Once you enter the Common, you'll see lines forming naturally. Each one looks longer than the next one, and no, you're not going to find a shorter, faster moving line.

Transportation: the only official way to get to Hopkinton on race morning is on these B.A.A. buses lined up on Tremont Street. The first bus leaves at 6:00am, and the last bus takes off at about 7:30.

A long line of buses filled with runners drive in formation to Hopkinton, roughly a 30 to 40 minute trip.

Athletes' Village. The Athletes' Village, available to official runners only from 6:30am to 10:00am.

Amenities. Oversized circus-like tents provide shelter on each field, and water, Gatorade, bagels, coffee and porto-potties are provided at many locations surrounding the fields.

First thing to do: find a spot in a tent or on the field. Spread out your stuff, then explore.

You'll have an hour or two before the race. When you're relaxing, pass the time engaging nearby runners.

Bib Numbers. Assigned based on your qualifying time, and the first non-elite bib number is #1001.

Wave Start. Wave 1, which starts the race at 10:00am with the elite men, is comprised of the top 10,000 or so runners. Wave 2, all the remaining runners, begins the race at 10:30.

Leaving Athletes' Village. Allow plenty of time leaving Hopkinton High School for the 0.7 mile walk to the starting line.

Bag Check. The bag check process is seamless, logical and fast. The first bus accepts bags for runner #1001 to #1500, second bus is for runners #1501 to #2000, and so on.

Meanwhile, elites are warming up in an alley near the start line under watchful eye of coaches.

The runners look loose and casual. But you know they are checking each other, wondering: Who'll win?

Start Corrals. Starting corrals – informal square holding pens, sort of – are formed to hold 1000 runners each. If your bib number is 9863, you are assigned to the 9th Corral, for example.

Race Start:
Hopkinton

Course Overview					Benchmark Splits		
Mile	City	Milestone	Elevation	Change	1996	1999	2002
Start	Hopkinton	Starting Line	490	n/a			
1	Hopkinton		360	-130	9:48	7:55	6:49
2	Ashland	Starting Line 1897 to 1923	320	-40	8:17	6:58	6:40
3	Ashland		285	-35	8:23	6:55	6:35
4	Ashland	Ashland Clock Tower	180	-65	8:26	6:56	6:32
5	Framingham		205	25	8:06	7:07	6:38
6	Framingham		180	-25	8:10	7:04	6:29
7	Framingham	Framingham Train Depot	155	-25	8:11	6:58	6:32
8	Natick		180	25	8:04	6:58	6:31
9	Natick		150	-30	8:12	7:01	6:36
10	Natick	Lake Cochituate	170	20	8:13	7:07	6:38
11	Natick	Natick Town Common	160	-10	8:29	7:14	6:40
12	Wellesley		165	-15	8:02	7:24	6:46
13	Wellesley	Wellesley College	145	-20	8:05	7:05	6:30
14	Wellesley	Downtown Wellesley	130	-15	8:24	7:12	6:34
15	Wellesley		160	30	8:26	7:20	6:40
16	Wellesley	Wellesley Hills	60	-100	8:16	7:08	6:34
17	Newton Lower Falls	90/128 Overpass	115	55	8:36	7:35	6:54
18	Newton	Newton Fire Station	145	30	8:46	7:36	6:44
19	West Newton	Johnny Kelley Statue	130	-15	8:56	7:34	6:47
20	Newton	Second Newton Hill	150	20	8:46	7:42	6:51
21	Newton	Heartbreak Hill	230	80	8:58	8:02	7:07
22	Brookline	Boston College	190	-40	8:41	7:37	6:36
23	Brookline	Cleveland Circle	95	-55	9:03	7:48	6:43
24	Brookline	Coolidge Corner	60	-35	8:39	7:31	6:31
25	Boston	Boston University	15	-45	8:33	7:36	6:39
26	Boston	Citgo Sign/Fenway Park	10	-5	8:00	7:23	6:34
26.2	Boston/Back Bay	Boylston St.	10	0	1:32	1:36	1:26
Finish					3:41:07	3:12:24	2:54:37

Main Street. Prepare to experience the greatest marathon there is.

Race Start Times: Mobility Impaired Division: 9:00 a.m.; Wheelchair Division: 9:22 a.m.; Elite Women's: 9:32 a.m.; Elite Men's and Wave 1: 10:00 a.m.; Wave 2: 10:30 a.m.

Thousands of spectators line the road, often packed 10-people deep. You have to arrive pretty early to stake out a prime spot, like the one above: 50-feet from the starting line.

At 9:32am, elite women get final instructions from race director Dave McGillivary.

At 9:35am, the elite women sprint onto the course. Kara Goucher in the lead.

And the crowd goes wild as the remaining elite women runners charge into the race of their lives.

At 9:58, the process is repeated, this time for elite men and 10,000+ Wave 1 runners.

At 10:00am, the B.A.A.'s Guy Morse fires the starting gun, and the race is on.

Ryan Hall, far right, immediately leans into the lead, glancing to assess other runners.

Race Timing. Just before the 'Start' stripe, a street-wide timing mat will record each runner's start time.

Finally, it's your turn to cross the starting line. Race wisely. And have fun.

Pass the landmark intersection of Ash and Main, and then you're into the thick of it.

Headphone Policy. Headphones are allowed but gently discouraged by the B.A.A. I wear headphones every year, and so do thousands of others.

Note the bib numbers reaching into the 12,000 range. These are the last runners of Wave 1, crossing the line less than 10 minutes behind the front runners.

A narrow street crowded with runners restricts room to pass. It will be a mile or two before things open up.

Awesome view from the media bleachers at the starting line: You've never seen anything like it.

Spectators are screaming and just ahead a stereo is blaring the Rocky Theme. Really.

The downhill grade is not as sharp as you might expect. But don't let it fool you.

Relief. Porto-johns are located at each water/Gatorade and first aid station.

Look far ahead, all you see are runners, one big rainbow of color veering left.

Yes, the road is actually gently inclining here. Not for long, though.

Beautiful surroundings.

Hydration: Spring water and Gatorade stations are set up at approximately every mile on the course.

Ashland:
Miles 2 to 4

Mile	City	Milestone	Elevation	Change	1996	1999	2002
Start	Hopkinton	Starting Line					
1	Hopkinton						
2	Ashland	Starting Line 1897 to 1923	320	-40	8:17	6:58	6:40
3	Ashland		265	-55	8:23	6:55	6:35
4	Ashland	Ashland Clock Tower	180	-85	8:26	6:56	6:32
5	Framingham						
6	Framingham						
7	Framingham	Framingham Train Depot					
8	Natick						
9	Natick						
10	Natick	Lake Cochituate					
11	Natick	Natick Town Common					
12	Wellesley						
13	Wellesley	Wellesley College					
14	Wellesley	Downtown Wellesley					
15	Wellesley						
16	Wellesley	Wellesley Hills					
17	Newton Lower Falls	95/128 Overpass					
18	Newton	Newton Fire Station					
19	West Newton	Johnny Kelley Statue					
20	Newton	Second Newton Hill					
21	Newton	Heartbreak Hill					
22	Brookline	Boston College					
23	Brookline	Cleveland Circle					
24	Brookline	Coolidge Corner					
25	Boston	Boston University					
26	Boston	Citgo Sign/Fenway Park					
26.2	Boston/Back Bay	Boylston St.					
Finish					3:41:07	3:12:24	2:54:37

These miles are nearly all slightly downhill. Make sure not to overdo it in your early race excitement.

Here's one of Ashland's short uphills. Be conservative, like Little Sis and Big Sis.

Into mile 3, spectators start to line the road again. High-five the kids.

As the sign says: May the Course Be With You.

The Ashland Clock Tower just before the mile 4 marker serves as a first notable landmark on the course.

Aid stations are staggered: a row of volunteers on the right offering water and Gatorade followed about 100 yards later by the same fluids offered on the left side of the road.

Framingham:
Miles 5 to 7

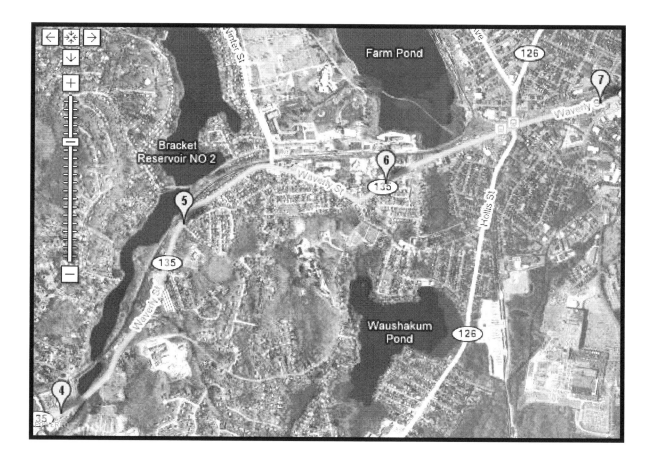

Course Overview					Benchmark Splits		
Mile	City	Milestone	Elevation	Change	1996	1999	2002
Start	Hopkinton	Starting Line	490	n/a			
1	Hopkinton		460	-30	9:43	7:05	6:15
2	Ashland	Starting Line 1897 & 1923	420	-40	8:17	6:58	6:44
3	Ashland		390	-30	8:23	6:55	6:26
4	Ashland	Ashland State Park	390	-5	8:26	6:56	6:32
5	Framingham		205	25	8:06	7:07	6:38
6	Framingham		180	-25	8:10	7:04	6:29
7	Framingham	Framingham Train Depot	155	-25	8:11	6:58	6:32
8	Natick		160	5	8:04	6:58	6:31
9	Natick		150	-10	8:02	7:01	6:16
10	Natick	Lake Cochituate	170	20	8:15	7:07	6:39
11	Natick	Natick Town Common	180	10	8:21	7:11	6:40
12	Wellesley		165	-15	8:02	7:24	6:46
13	Wellesley	Wellesley College	145	-20	8:09	7:05	6:39
14	Wellesley	Downtown Wellesley	130	-15	8:21	7:12	6:34
15	Wellesley		160	30	8:26	7:20	6:40
16	Wellesley	Wellesley Hills	60	-100	8:16	7:08	6:34
17	Newton Lower Falls	SR 128 Overpass	115	55	8:35	7:38	6:54
18	Newton	Newton Fire Station	145	30	8:46	7:36	6:44
19	Newton		130	-15	8:36	7:34	6:17
20	Newton	Second Newton Hill	160	30	8:46	7:42	6:51
21	Newton	Heartbreak Hill	230	80	8:56	8:02	7:07
22	Brookline	Boston College	150	-80	8:41	7:37	6:53
23	Brookline	Cleveland Circle	95	-55	9:05	7:46	6:43
24	Brookline	Coolidge Corner	60	-35	8:32	7:34	6:31
25	Boston	Boston University	15	-45	8:21	7:35	6:59
26	Boston	Citgo Sign/Fenway Park	10	-5	8:00	7:23	6:34
26.2	Boston/Back Bay	Boylston St.	10	0	1:32	1:38	1:28
Finish					3:41:07	3:12:24	2:54:37

Overview: Framingham

Your goal on these three Framingham miles is to run each one at about the same pace; see my splits below. A promising pace will be around the same or slightly slower pace than you ran in Ashland, see 1998, 1999, 2002.

Miles 5 and 6 approaching this destination have continued to roll gently downhill with some brief inclines, but by now you're under control. The net course elevation change is 50 feet, but it won't strike you as a distinctive change in one place or another. It's the course settling into a groove, as you are.

The main landmark in Framingham is the train station and large crowds greeting runners at about the 6.4 mile point.

Enjoy the crowd in Framingham -- wave, smile, soak in all the adulation. You won't see many people for three more miles after that.

Interesting to note that in each year of data below, my Framingham miles were at nearly the exact pace. Try it.

Incredibly inspiring: disabled athlete uses feet to push backward for all 26.2 miles.

And the sign said: Runner's High -- Legal in All 50 States.

Bright sky, open road, the train station is just ahead.

The station, at 6.4 miles, is a good check point: how do you feel? Strong? Good.

On the way out of town, get water. I stop at every other aid station for a full cup.

Natick:
Miles 8 to 11

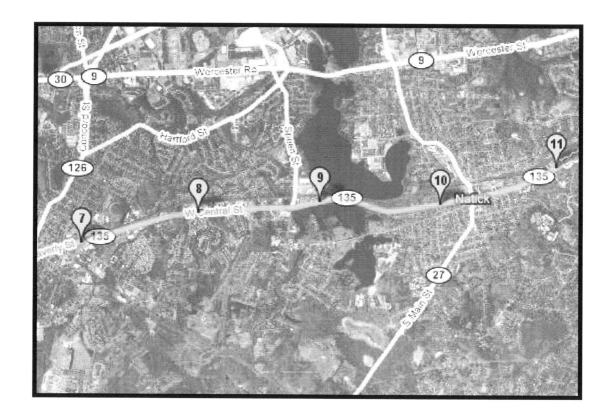

Course Overview					Benchmark Splits		
Mile	City	Milestone	Elevation	Change	1996	1999	2002
Start	Hopkinton	Starting Line	490	0			
1	Hopkinton		460	-30	8:08	7:58	7:11
2	Ashland	Starting Line 1897 to 1923	320	-40	8:17	7:18	6:40
3	Ashland		265	-55		6:19	6:43
4	Ashland	Ashland Clock Tower	180	-85	8:25	5:58	6:32
5	Framingham		225	25	8:04	6:27	6:29
6	Framingham		180	-25	8:10	7:04	6:29
7	Framingham	Framingham Train Depot	155	-25	8:11	6:58	6:32
8	Natick		180	25	8:04	6:58	6:31
9	Natick		150	-30	8:02	7:01	6:36
10	Natick	Lake Cochituate	170	20	8:13	7:07	6:39
11	Natick	Natick Town Common	180	10	8:24	7:14	6:40
12	Wellesley		155	-25	8:10	7:24	6:41
13	Wellesley	Wellesley College	145	-10	8:04	7:05	6:30
14	Wellesley	Downtown Wellesley	130	-15	8:24	7:12	6:34
15	Wellesley		160	30	8:29	7:20	6:48
16	Wellesley	Wellesley Hills	60	-100	8:15	7:06	6:34
17	Newton Lower Falls	95/128 Overpass	115	55	8:49	7:35	6:54
18	Newton	Newton Fire Station	145	30	8:48	7:56	6:44
19	West Newton	Johnny Kelley Statue	130	-15	9:18	7:34	6:47
20	Newton	Second Newton Hill	150	20	8:18	7:42	6:51
21	Newton	Heartbreak Hill	230	30	9:59	8:02	7:02
22	Brookline	Boston College	130	-60	8:11	7:37	7:01
23	Brookline	Cleveland Circle	75	-35	8:08	7:46	6:41
24	Brookline	Coolidge Corner	60	-15	8:02	7:24	6:42
25	Boston	Boston University	10	-40	8:23	7:56	6:39
26	Boston	Citgo Sign/Fenway Park	10	0	8:00	7:41	6:34
26.2	Boston/Back Bay	Boylston St.	10	0	6:12	11:06	4:56
Finish					3:41:07	3:12:24	2:54:37

Overview: Natick

The first three Natick miles are quiet, and some peace on the road at this point is exactly what you need.

After all the excitement from early morning through the first few miles, now it's time to do what you do best: run. The course is calm, gently rolling, but not difficult.

Near the 15k mark, you run between two calm ponds; some noise is not far ahead. After 10 miles, you enter downtown Natick, with a prominent church as a landmark.

Crowds will be waiting at Main Street, waving you on your way to Wellesley. After Natick, the next mile always seems to slow me down a little. See data below.

Stay in control and appreciate your surroundings.

Because when you get to Wellesley, the real race really starts.

Natick's attempt to make some noise: This is what 100% sounds like.

A great sight: senior citizens line the road, top hats optional, to cheer.

The most scenic spot on the course, Lake Cochituate, just past the 9-mile mark.

Sign = Victory's Not Sweet in Boston. It's Salty.

Athlete Tracking. Every 5k, timing mats record your progress and uploads it to baa.org.

The road is specially painted for your photo opportunity. Cameras ahead.

Race Photos. Smile, it's portrait time. Let the photographers see how well you're running.

After a little 15k and photo excitement, back to running a couple more quiet miles.

You'll then enter downtown Natick, loaded with cheering spectators.

The church is Natick's main landmark on the course. It also means: Wellesley soon.

Wellesley
Miles 12 to 15

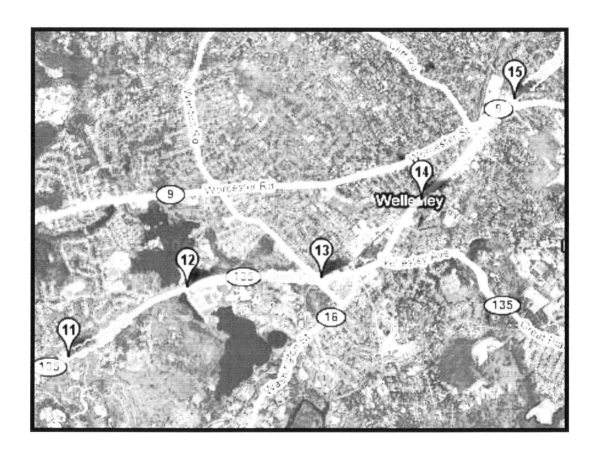

Mile	City	Milestone	Elevation	Change	1996	1999	2002
Start	Hopkinton	Starting Line	490	n/e			
1	Hopkinton		360	-130	9:48	7:55	6:49
2	Ashland	Starting Line 1897 to 1923	320	-40	8:17	6:58	6:40
3	Ashland		265	-55	8:23	6:55	6:35
4	Ashland	Ashland Clock Tower	180	-85	8:26	6:56	6:32
5	Framingham		205	25	8:06	7:07	6:38
6	Framingham		180	-25	8:10	7:04	6:29
7	Framingham	Framingham Train Depot	155	-25	8:11	6:58	6:32
8	Natick		180	25	8:04	6:58	6:31
9	Natick		150	-30	8:02	7:01	6:26
10	Natick	Lake Cochituate	170	20	8:13	7:07	6:39
11	Natick	Natick Town Common	180	10	8:24	7:14	6:40
12	Wellesley		165	-15	8:02	7:24	6:46
13	Wellesley	Wellesley College	145	-20	8:05	7:05	6:30
14	Wellesley	Downtown Wellesley	130	-15	8:24	7:12	6:34
15	Wellesley		160	30	8:26	7:20	6:40
16	Wellesley	Wellesley Hills	60	-100	8:16	7:08	6:34
17	Newton Lower Falls	95/128 Overpass	115	55	8:35	7:35	6:54
18	Newton	Newton Fire Station	145	30	8:46	7:36	6:44
19	West Newton	Johnny Kelley Statue	130	-15	8:36	7:34	6:47
20	Newton	Second Newton Hill	150	20	8:45	7:42	6:51
21	Newton	Heartbreak Hill	230	80	8:58	8:02	7:07
22	Brookline	Boston College	150	-80	8:41	7:37	6:36
23	Brookline	Cleveland Circle	95	-55	9:03	7:48	6:43
24	Brookline	Coolidge Corner	60	-35	8:32	7:34	6:31
25	Boston	Boston University	15	-45	8:23	7:35	6:39
26	Boston	Citgo Sign/Fenway Park	10	-5	8:00	7:23	6:34
26.2	Boston/Back Bay	Boylston St.	10	0	1:32	1:36	1:28
Finish					3:41:07	3:12:24	2:54:37

Overview: Wellesley

The Wellesley miles are miles of transition, where a controlled run becomes a race. But first, there is nothing like the Screaming Women of Wellesley College.

Sure, you've read about them, but you have to be there to experience it. The screaming is so overpowering, in a fun way, that I steered clear left away from all the fuss in my first few Boston Marathons.

But in recent years, I've decided to join the fun, running close to the crowd, taking it all in. You should too.

Because after that, it's all uphill. Sort of.

The 13.1 mile point in town is gut-check time. Then you veer left toward the rest of the race. The miles become increasingly challenging on your way out of Wellesley, see below. You'll be tested; try to hold form and speed.

Brace Your Ears.

Another 5k down, 12.4 miles done. The volume of Wellesley College is near.

Suddenly -- hold on to your hat, get your earplugs, it's Screaming Time.

Go ahead, accept the cheers and slap a few hands. You're great, they tell you. Agree.

Runners looking for 'Kiss Me' sign-holders. The 'Keep It Up' one doesn't count.

OK, here the kisses are requested. Be polite, mind your manners, live a little.

Just past the College, reality sets in at the 13.1 mile point. Halfway done. Feeling ok?

Downtown Wellesley. Prepare to dig into the hard part. Hold on for a wild ride.

Newton
Miles 16 to 21

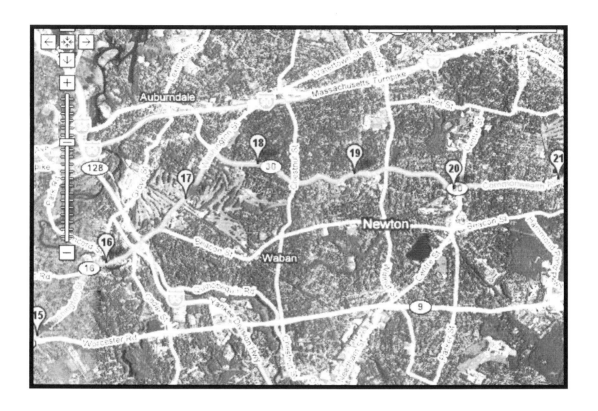

Mile	City	Milestone	Elevation	Change	1996	1999	2002
Start	Hopkinton	Starting Line	490	n/a			
1	Hopkinton		360	-130	9:49	7:55	6:49
2	Ashland	Starting Line 1897 to 1923	320	-40	8:17	6:58	6:40
3	Ashland		265	-55	8:23	6:55	6:35
4	Ashland	Ashland Clock Tower	180	-85	8:28	6:56	6:32
5	Framingham		205	25	8:06	7:07	6:38
6	Framingham		180	-25	8:10	7:04	6:29
7	Framingham	Framingham Train Depot	155	-25	8:11	6:58	6:32
8	Natick		180	25	8:04	6:59	6:31
9	Natick		150	-30	8:02	7:01	6:36
10	Natick	Lake Cochituate	170	20	8:13	7:07	6:39
11	Natick	Natick Town Common	180	10	8:24	7:14	6:40
12	Wellesley		165	-15	8:02	7:24	6:46
13	Wellesley	Wellesley College	145	-20	8:05	7:05	6:30
14	Wellesley	Downtown Wellesley	130	-15	8:24	7:12	6:34
15	Wellesley		160	30	8:26	7:20	6:40
16	Wellesley	Wellesley Hills	60	-100	8:16	7:08	6:34
17	Newton Lower Falls	95/128 Overpass	115	55	8:35	7:35	6:54
18	Newton	Newton Fire Station	145	30	8:46	7:36	6:44
19	West Newton	Johnny Kelley Statue	130	-15	8:36	7:34	6:47
20	Newton	Second Newton Hill	150	20	8:45	7:42	6:51
21	Newton	Heartbreak Hill	230	80	8:56	8:02	7:07
22	Brookline	Boston College	150	-80	8:41	7:37	6:36
23	Brookline	Cleveland Circle	95	-55	8:03	7:46	6:43
24	Brookline	Coolidge Corner	60	-35	8:32	7:34	6:31
25	Boston	Boston University	15	-45	8:23	7:36	6:39
26	Boston	Citgo Sign/Fenway Park	10	-5	8:00	7:23	6:34
26.2	Boston/Back Bay	Boylston St.	10	0	1:32	1:38	1:28
Finish					3:41:07	3:12:24	2:54:37

Overview: Newton

The heart of the race passes through Newton; buckle up:

1.   Mile 16-17: Newton 95/128 Overpass
2.   Mile 18: Fire Station Hill
3.   Mile 19-20: Hill # 2
4.   Mile 21: Heartbreak Hill

The key sections of the Newton miles are detailed on the next few pages.

My splits below tell the tale: my race thrives or dies in Newton. So will yours.

Remember: your performance in Newton has everything to do with the strategy that got you to this point. Hope your strategy was a good one.

You Are Here. Heading into the eye of the storm. Think positive.

Overview: Miles 16-17 Newton 95/128 Overpass

The tough hills of the Boston Marathon really begin just after the 16 mile mark.

There's a solid incline as the road approaches and crosses the 95/128 freeway.

The spectators will begin narrowing to see runners, until there's a small gap to run through as you cross the bridge.

They will be telling you 'you look great!' but you will begin wondering if you can handle the rest of the hills. Be confident: sure you can.

But you may prepare yourself to run mile 17 about 20 to 30 seconds slower than mile 16. Simple: 16 is downhill, 17 goes up.

Follow the 95 North sign. Just don't take the exit ramp. Follow the crowd.

You'll start to see signs of fatigue on the bridge. More to come.

Just east of the 95/128 overpass. Steady pace for the next mile, then prepare to work.

Overview Mile 18: Newton Fire Station Hill

Keep running under control, and when you see the crowds getting thicker, prepare for a solid right hand turn at the Newton Fire Station to begin a steady climb.

The crowds will cheer, you will smile as you put your head down and chug up this hill. It's about 3/8 of a mile long, not too terrible.

I just run at the side of the road, keeping my eyes on the white stripe on the road, not looking for the top.

When I get there, I get there. And when you reach the top of that hill, again a surprise awaits. It's more than a mile to the next hill, and most of that is downhill, to boot.

In fact, by this time, you will begin wondering what all this talk about the Hills of Boston was all about. Just wait.

Between your excitement and the screaming crowd you may miss it: the fire station.

But you'll know where you are by the hill, up ahead. Focus.

And the fun begins. I tend to run on the left side to concentrate: a stride at a time.

Running on the line, just follow it to the top.

Well, maybe slap the hands of a few well-wishers. Be their hero today.

A cop rides crowd control on the left, breaking concentration for a moment.

This is what the road sees: determined runners. You are one of them. Keep driving.

You're wondering: are we nearing the end of this one?

Yes . . . in 100 yards or so, the course tapers downward. Just in time.

Looking back: yes, you just took that hill.

Overview: Mile 19-20 Newton Hill #2

Your main challenge at this point will be similar to your other marathons: handling getting through mile 19 with enough left in your tank to finish.

Even though it's a theoretically easy mile, 19 is tough. The next Newton Hill arrives at about mile 19.25, and is a little deceptive.

Not particularly steep, it just keeps going longer than you expect. At 19.5, you will think you've crested the climb, but it's a brief respite.

There's more to go. Stay with it. Try to not blow up as I did in 2001.

Remember, I started way too fast that year; payback time hits hard at mile 20 if you're not ready.

If you can keep your mile 20 time within 15-20 seconds of your mile 19 split, you're doing well.

The 30k timing mat. 18.6 miles done, 7.6 to go. Even if you have to shuffle.

Once again, the camera crew. Try to look happy. Then enjoy some flat road ahead.

Behind you, the pack of runners has really thinned out.

More spectators become the telling sign: you're approaching the next challenge.

Note the landmark, the church. About the mile 19 point, good to know.

Make sure you take water at this aid station. Really important, you'll need it.

And then it begins again. A long, gentle looking incline. Harder than it looks.

More runners are clearly hurting at this point. Offer encouragement and a smile.

Looks like a very reasonable incline. Careful. Don't underestimate it.

Unless you're a Superhero carrying a torch with special climbing powers.

Heat and hills are not the best combination for some runners. Be careful out there.

The fallen runner was well cared-for; other racers continue toward the top of the hill.

Self-portrait of the author approaching Heartbreak Hill (see sleeve, right).

This runner delights friends with a group photo just steps before Heartbreak Hill.

Overview: Mile 21 Newton Heartbreak Hill

Then, you're at the 20 mile marker. 10k to go, the fun part. But a last challenge awaits: Heartbreak. You will hear the climb before you actually get there. The roar of the crowd, combined with a pounding of drums, tells you that It's Almost Here.

See the gentle turn ahead, you will veer in that direction, then you will encounter an incline that simply disappears into the trees above. You will not see the top. Keep your head down, stay focused on the road. Tell yourself that in a few very short minutes it will be over, and you'll be on your way to the finish.

When you get near the top, you will know it. Literally, a clearing seems to open up, and you can begin to see daylight. After a small dip, which you'll hope signals the end, there's another small incline then the hard part is over.

You're on top of the backside of the course, and you'll be able to see downtown Boston in the distance, just before you fly (or not) downhill towards Boston College.

Then assess the damage: Heartbreak Hill beats me most times; I won the battle in 2002.

Spectators lean in to wish runners good luck at the foot of Heartbreak Hill.

Good wishes accepted, runners dig in as they begin the ascent.

Yes, it's as steep as it looks. And it looks like it goes on forever.

Adapt your stride as necessary, to maintain a good pace.

Sometimes sharing the climb with a nearby runner makes it easier.

On and on, and yes, it's still that steep.

Heartbreak doesn't check ID cards, but age is just a number after all.

If you need to walk, walk. Saving some strength here may make you faster later.

There seems to be a clearing ahead . . . you'll be wondering if you're almost there.

At the top, there's a deceiving short flat section, then another sharp incline.

But the final incline is short. When you see sponsor tents, you're at the top. Nice.

It's downhill from here, sort of. The 21 mile marker at Boston College. 5.2 to go.

Brookline
Miles 22 to 24

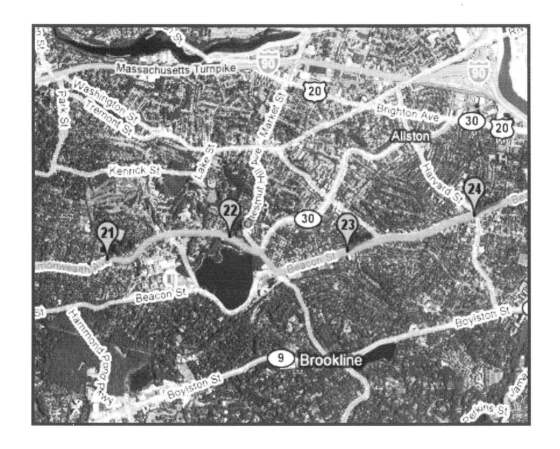

Mile	City	Milestone	Elevation	Change	1996	1999	2002
Start	Hopkinton	Starting Line	490	n/a			
1	Hopkinton		360	-130	9:48	7:55	6:49
2	Ashland	Starting Line 1897 to 1923	320	-40	8:17	6:58	6:40
3	Ashland		265	-55	8:23	6:55	6:35
4	Ashland	Ashland Clock Tower	180	-85	8:26	6:56	6:32
5	Framingham		205	25	8:06	7:07	6:35
6	Framingham		180	-25	8:10	7:04	6:29
7	Framingham	Framingham Train Depot	155	-25	8:11	6:58	6:32
8	Natick		180	25	8:04	6:58	6:31
9	Natick		150	-30	8:02	7:01	6:36
10	Natick	Lake Cochituate	170	20	8:13	7:07	6:39
11	Natick	Natick Town Common	180	10	8:24	7:14	6:40
12	Wellesley		165	-15	8:02	7:24	6:46
13	Wellesley	Wellesley College	145	-20	8:05	7:05	6:30
14	Wellesley	Downtown Wellesley	130	-15	8:24	7:12	6:34
15	Wellesley		160	30	8:26	7:20	6:40
16	Wellesley	Wellesley Hills	60	-100	8:16	7:08	6:34
17	Newton Lower Falls	95/128 Overpass	115	55	8:35	7:35	6:54
18	Newton	Newton Fire Station	145	30	8:46	7:36	6:44
19	West Newton	Johnny Kelley Statue	130	-15	8:36	7:34	6:47
20	Newton	Second Newton Hill	150	20	8:45	7:42	6:51
21	Newton	Heartbreak Hill	230	80	8:58	8:02	7:07
22	Brookline	Boston College	150	-80	8:41	7:37	6:36
23	Brookline	Cleveland Circle	95	-55	9:03	7:48	6:43
24	Brookline	Coolidge Corner	60	-35	8:32	7:34	6:31
25	Boston	Boston University	15	-45	8:23	7:35	6:39
26	Boston	Citgo Sign/Fenway Park	10	-5	8:00	7:23	6:34
26.2	Boston/Back Bay	Boylston St.	10	0	1:32	1:36	1:28
Finish					3:41:07	3:12:24	2:54:37

Overview: Brookline

Miles 22, 23 and 24 on their way though Brookline towards Boston are each net downhill, but that doesn't mean the course won't toss you a slight curveball here and there.

After 22, the course takes you down to Cleveland Circle, then you'll run alongside the Green Line trains toward Boston. You'll encounter several gentle inclines that frustrate the mind and body ever so irritatingly.

As my body is wearing down in those final miles, I start thinking that the finish line can't come soon enough.

And these little jabs by the very slight course inclines seem much more potent than they should be. But you're getting closer to the finish with each step.

Try to keep relatively consistent pace for these three miles.

Perfect timing: a much-needed aid station at Boston College's gates. Drink up.

Mind Over Body; Body Over Hill.

Mile 23, the Green Line alongside runners. Taking the train home seems tempting.

Brookline Village. Beautiful view of the finish line area, three miles ahead.

Brain OFF. Legs ON. If you've got speed left in your legs, time to get going.

Boston
Miles 25 to 26.2

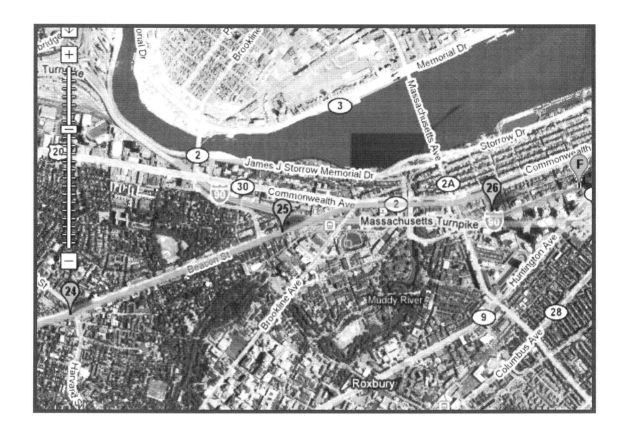

184

Course Overview					Benchmark Splits		
Mile	City	Milestone	Elevation	Change	1996	1999	2002
Start	Hopkinton	Starting Line	490	n/a			
1	Hopkinton		360	-130	9:48	7:55	6:49
2	Ashland	Starting Line 1897 to 1923	320	-40	8:17	6:58	6:40
3	Ashland		265	-55	8:23	6:55	6:35
4	Ashland	Ashland Clock Tower	180	-85	8:26	6:58	6:32
5	Framingham		205	25	8:06	7:07	6:38
6	Framingham		180	-25	8:10	7:04	6:29
7	Framingham	Framingham Train Depot	155	-25	8:11	6:58	6:32
8	Natick		180	25	8:04	6:58	6:31
9	Natick		150	-30	8:02	7:01	6:36
10	Natick	Lake Cochituate	170	20	8:13	7:07	6:39
11	Natick	Natick Town Common	180	10	8:24	7:14	6:40
12	Wellesley		165	-15	8:02	7:24	6:46
13	Wellesley	Wellesley College	145	-20	8:05	7:05	6:30
14	Wellesley	Downtown Wellesley	130	-15	8:24	7:12	6:34
15	Wellesley		160	30	8:26	7:20	6:40
16	Wellesley	Wellesley Hills	60	-100	8:16	7:08	6:34
17	Newton Lower Falls	95/128 Overpass	115	55	8:35	7:35	6:54
18	Newton	Newton Fire Station	145	30	8:46	7:36	6:44
19	West Newton	Johnny Kelley Statue	130	-15	8:36	7:34	6:47
20	Newton	Second Newton Hill	150	20	8:45	7:42	6:51
21	Newton	Heartbreak Hill	230	80	8:56	8:02	7:07
22	Brookline	Boston College	150	-80	8:41	7:37	6:36
23	Brookline	Cleveland Circle	95	-55	9:03	7:46	6:43
24	Brookline	Coolidge Corner	60	-35	8:32	7:34	6:31
25	Boston	Boston University	15	-45	8:23	7:35	6:39
26	Boston	Citgo Sign/Fenway Park	10	-5	8:00	7:23	6:34
26.2	Boston/Back Bay	Boylston St.	10	0	1:32	1:36	1:26
Finish					3:41:07	3:12:24	2:54:37

Passing Boston University and approaching mile 25 you can begin to feel the finish line.

The Citgo sign in the distance is the beacon, the 25 mile point.

After you cross a final incline over the Mass Pike, start thinking about your finish, keep running strong.

Here it is: Citgo. Yes, it's happening. You're close to finishing Boston. Believe it.

One Mile to Go. It's an amazing feeling.

Suddenly the course seems to open up. A few moments to run alone.

The final big sign: Boston is Everything – Impossible is Nothing. Absolutely.

Commonwealth Ave., Back Bay. Note road sign: veer left to get to the finish line.

A new element has been added to the final mile in recent years: the Mass. Ave. underpass.

Merely a slight diversion. Coming out the other side, you'll begin to hear the crowd.

You are on hallowed ground, following the footsteps of more than 100 years of marathoners.

If you're feeling good at this point, you can run the last mile faster. Right onto Hereford St.

The left turn onto Boylston is just ahead. The finish line is on Boylston. Your finish line.

The turn onto Boylston Street, then the greatest final stretch that you can experience in a marathon.

The finish banner, an unparalleled sight, comes into view.

Nearly a half-mile of smiles waves and cheers from spectators on both sides of the street.

When you cross that line, you join a special club of Boston Finishers.

See the time, cross the line, smile for the cameras. You've done it.

Finish

You've done it. Go ahead, admit it to yourself: you Really Rock. You're a Boston Finisher. Yes, you are.

You've done something extraordinary, celebrate it. Celebrate your independence, celebrate your spirit and attitude that earned that trip to Hopkinton and drove you the next 26.2 miles to the most coveted finisher's medal in long-distance running.

In the Long Run, life is a collection of Moments That Matter. The ones you will remember for the rest of your life. In April, your moment is in Boston, on Boylston Street, under the Finish Banner.

That moment is yours. Celebrate it. From that moment on, you are a little more special. You are Boston finisher. Congratulations. Welcome to the Club.

206

209

211

212

Appendix: Race Entry, Qualifying Times, Race Week Schedule and Watching the Race

Boston Marathon Race Entry

Registration for the Boston Marathon usually begins late summer of the year before the race. Qualified entrants may register for the race from that date through late February, or when the limit of 25,000 runners is reached, whichever is sooner.

In the not-too-distant past, Boston did not sell out before the end of the registration period. This meant that mid-February races like the Houston Marathon became favorite last-minute destinations for those who wanted to get a qualifying time and enter before the cutoff date. Those days are long gone.

Registration for the 2010 Boston Marathon opened on September 8 and the race sold out by late November 2009, earlier than ever. Expect next year's entry to close earlier, and plan your qualifying race date accordingly.

An alternative path to securing entry into Boston is to participate with one of the charitable foundations that offer entry in return for fund-raising commitments.

Qualifying for Boston Marathon

To qualify, runners must meet or beat the designated time standard that corresponds to their age group.

Age Group	Men	Women
18-34	3hrs 10min	3hrs 40min
35-39	3hrs 15min	3hrs 45min
40-44	3hrs 20min	3hrs 50min
45-49	3hrs 30min	4hrs 00min
50-54	3hrs 35min	4hrs 05min
55-59	3hrs 45min	4hrs 15min
60-64	4hrs 00min	4hrs 30min
65-69	4hrs 15min	4hrs 45min
70-74	4hrs 30min	5hrs 00min
75-79	4hrs 45min	5hrs 15min
80 and older	5hrs 00min	5hrs 30min

An extra 59 seconds may be allowed in addition to each designated time. Example: a 36 year-old man who runs a 3:15:29 qualifies under this rule.

Age on race day, e.g., April 19, 2010 determines qualifying time. If your age will be 40 on April 18, for example, you can qualify against the M40-44 time, even if you run your qualifying race earlier, at age 39.

The wide qualifying window – typically the from the October 18 months before race day through February of Race Year – means that a qualifying run in one year may make you eligible for two Boston Marathons. For more, see bostonmarathon.com.

Race Week Schedule

114th Boston Marathon Number Pick-Up and
John Hancock Sports and Fitness Expo

- Friday 4/16/10 2:00 p.m. – 7:00 p.m.
- Saturday 4/17/10 9:00 a.m. – 6:00 p.m.
- Sunday 4/18/10 9:00 a.m. – 6:00 p.m.

Location: John B. Hynes Veterans Memorial Convention Center
900 Boylston Street, Boston

B.A.A. Youth Relay Challenge
Saturday 4/17/10 11:00 a.m. – 1:00 p.m.
Copley Square Park, Boston

B.A.A. 5K
Sunday 4/18/10 8:00 a.m.
Boylston Street - At Boston Public Library

B.A.A. Invitational Miles and Youth Races
Sunday 4/18/10 9:30 a.m. (following the conclusion of the B.A.A. 5K)
Boylston Street – At Boston Public Library

Boston Marathon Pre-Race Dinner
Sunday 4/18/10 4:30 p.m. – 8:00 p.m.
City Hall Plaza, Boston

The pre-race dinner is the best chance for runners to load up with a big meal before the Boston Marathon. Official entrants and guests are invited. Runners are assigned a certain time for being seated.

Monday, April 19, 2010 (Race Day)

Transportation to Start
6:00 to 7:30 a.m.
Tremont Street side of the Boston Common in Boston's Back Bay area:

- 6:00 a.m.–6:45 a.m. Bib #'s 1,000–13,999
- 6:45 a.m.–7:30 a.m. Bib #'s 14,000+

B.A.A. Athletes' Village
6:30 a.m. – 10:00 a.m.
Hopkinton High School, Hopkinton

Official entrants only. Entertainment, light refreshments, Poland Spring water, Gatorade Endurance
Formula, tenting, and portable toilets will be available.

114ᵗʰ Boston Marathon

- 9:00 a.m. Start of Mobility Impaired Program
- 9:17 a.m. Start of Handcycle Participants
- 9:22 a.m. Start of Push Rim Wheelchair Division
- 9:32 a.m. Start of Elite Women's Race
- 10:00 a.m. Start of Elite Men's Race and Wave One of the 114th Boston Marathon
- 10:30 a.m. Start of Wave Two of the 114th Boston Marathon

Boston Marathon Awards Ceremony
5:00 p.m.
Grand Ballroom - Fairmont Copley Plaza Hotel
The champions and top age-division finishers will receive their awards.

Watching the Race: Where, When and How to get There

Commuter Rail

Station	Mile
Ashland	3.7
Framingham	6.6
West Natick	8.0
Natick	10.0
Wellesley Square	13.4
Wellesley Hills	14.4
Wellesley Farms	15.5
Back Bay	Finish Area

MTBA Green Line

Station	Mile
Woodland (D Line)	16.8
Boston College (B Line)	21.4
Cleveland Circle - St. Mary's (C Line)	23.0
Kenmore (B,C, D Lines)	25.2
Hynes Convention Center (B, C, D Lines)	25.5

Estimate of Race Leaders' Time Schedule

Stage	Location	M Wheel	W Wheel	Women	Men
Start	Main St., Hopkinton	9:17am	9:17am	9:32am	10:00am
5k	Rte. 135, Ashland	9:26am	9:26am	9:49am	10:15am
10k	Rte. 135, Framingham	9:36am	9:38am	10:06am	10:30am
15k	Rte. 135, Natick	9:47am	9:50am	10:22am	10:46am
20k	Rte. 135, Wellesley	9:57am	10:02am	10:39am	11:01am
Half Marathon	Rte. 135, Wellesley	9:59am	10:04am	10:42am	11:04am
25k	Rte. 16, Wellesley	10:07am	10:14am	10:57am	11:16am
30k	Rte. 30, Newton	10:17am	10:26am	11:14am	11:31am
35k	Rte. 30, Boston	10:27am	10:38am	11:31am	11:47am
40k	Beacon St., Boston	10:36am	10:49am	11:48am	12:02pm
Finish	Boylston St., Boston	10:41am	10:55am	11:56am	12:08pm

About the Author

Raymond Britt is Managing Partner at WinSight Ventures, publisher of RunTri.com and one of the most experienced endurance athletes in the world.

Few can match Britt's extensive competitive record. He's completed 29 Ironman Triathlons (2.4 mile swim, 112 mile bike ride, 26.2 mile run), 48 Marathons, 8 Ultramarathons (31 miles or longer) and more than 60 other triathlons and running races.

Since his debut race – the 1994 Chicago Marathon – Britt has covered nearly 50,000 training and racing miles around the globe. He's finished the Chicago Marathon 12 times, the Boston Marathon 13 consecutive times, Hawaii Ironman World Championships 3 times, and has been a USA Triathlon All-American.

Britt's articles, photographs and perspectives have been featured by CNN, NBC, New York Times, USA Today, Chicago Tribune, Chicago Sun-Times, Los Angeles Times, Triathlete magazine, Running Times magazine and many others.

As publisher of RunTri.com, Britt serves an annual audience of 500,000 worldwide readers, providing free training and racing resources to help athletes achieve their goals.

Made in the USA
Lexington, KY
12 January 2015